The Funeral

A Chance to Touch
A Chance to Serve
A Chance to Heal

by Doug Manning

In-Sight Books

1st printing–January 2001

Copyright© 2001 by In-Sight Books, Inc.
P. O. Box 42467
Oklahoma City, Oklahoma 73123
1-800-658-9262
www.insightbooks.com

Manufactured in the United States of America

ISBN 1-892785-37-4

Cover: *A Time for Remembering* by Carl J. Smith

Dedicated To

Arnold Dodge

Funeral Service has never had a better
friend, and neither have I.

"We" Squared

I love to write in the first person. I like to talk about *you, me, us* and *we* instead of the normal *they* or some professional title. This makes my books seem more personal and warm. That has never been a problem until I started writing this book.

I was a pastor for thirty-seven years, so when I talk about the clergy I am a "we".

I have always been deeply involved in the funeral process. My best friend in high school worked at a funeral home and became a mortician. I spent many nights of my youth hanging out with him among the dead. In my pastorates I was always good friends with the funeral directors. I have helped them embalm, make ambulance runs, and go to the home to remove the body when a death happened. For a brief time, I was part owner of a funeral home. When I talk about funeral directors I am a "we".

Welcome to the world of "We" squared.

Table of Contents

Section I
The Value of the Funeral

CHAPTER 1

The Value of a Funeral

I have watched the movement away from the traditional funeral with a deepening sense of sorrow and foreboding. There is a growing perception that the funeral is barbaric and plastic, and that funeral directors are charlatans preying on families when they are the most vulnerable. The idea seems to be that since a person can be buried in a cardboard box, anything more than that is a waste of money and a rip-off. Articles blasting funeral service appear in major publications on an increasingly regular basis. These articles take the most extreme examples possible and pass them off as the norm. Publications that have always held themselves to a high standard for reporting are now willing to use the same type of writing as the muckraking tabloids in order to blast the funeral profession.

There is also a growing perception that sophisticated people are somehow above the need for a public expression of grief. It is considered "more civilized" to take care of such things in a more private manner. The loved one is quietly "disposed" of with no fuss. Anything else is considered gauché and undignified.

I wish Jackie Kennedy had cried at her husband's funeral. We have the image of her standing on the steps of the capital in stoic silence while John John saluted his father. The whole world gushed about how strong she was, and talked about how much dignity and sophistication she showed in her dealing with this tragic death. That has become our model. Classy people don't cry. Dignity allows for no public showing of grief. To cry is a sign of weakness. To really break down is just not done in cultured circles.

I have not only observed these perceptions as they developed, I have lived with the results. My brother died and disappeared. His body was removed from the emergency room within minutes of his death and transferred to a crematorium where he was cremated. No one saw him after his death. A few days later we gathered in a military chapel on the base where he served and held a twenty minute memorial service. The service had to be done in twenty minutes because an honor guard was to present the military ceremony at the end. When the service was over we moved to the officer's club for a cocktail party.

I had to officiate at my brother's funeral. I did not want to do that, but there was no one else. He had no church affiliation and no clergy person to call. Someone remarked that doing the service must have been one of the hardest things I have ever been called upon to do. I responded that it was not hard at all, but I wish it had been. We gathered together to act like no one had died. The whole service was a process of denial. My mother did not shed a tear at her son's funeral.

The cocktail party was strained and unreal. I expected this to be different than other such parties, but it was not. We stood around and made small talk denying that anything had happened.

My brother wanted this kind of service because he was convinced that this would be easier on his family. A leading columnist wrote recently that his friend had chosen this kind of service instead of the "normal three hanky jobs that are so hard on the family." That is the current perception and that is how my brother saw it.

My brother was right. It was easier on the family. Denial is always easier than reality. The funeral itself was not hard at all. Had he chosen a normal funeral there would have been much more crying and more public display. But to determine if this is truly easier on the family we must look beyond the service itself. We must determine whether or not this time of denial makes it easier for the family to walk through the grieving process. If not, then the choice is between an easier time on the day of the funeral, and more difficulty in the days to follow.

I still wish I could have had a time of saying good-bye to my brother. I can identify with some of the feelings of the families who have loved ones missing in action. They just disappeared and left an empty place that we find harder to fill because of the lack of closure and good-byes.

My brother's wife died within four years of her husband. Until almost the day of her death she was still calling me in the middle of the night crying about her loss.

Her grief was still as fresh as it was the days after the funeral. When the denial could hold no longer and she had to face the loss, she found it much harder to do than most of the people I deal with. That could have been caused by other factors of course, but from the many late night calls we shared I grew more and more convinced that a good part of her problem was based on his disappearing. I have nothing against cremation. I have a lot of things against making bodies disappear.

I have been deeply involved with the grieving process for almost thirty years. My interest started when I realized that as a minister I was totally ignorant about the grieving process and that I was doing a very bad job helping people through their grief. A young couple's daughter died suddenly and the mother was hysterical. Her husband and the doctor were trying to get her to calm down. She stepped back and said, "Don't take my grief away from me, I deserve it and I am going to have it." That statement went through me like a knife. I realized that was what I had been doing. That was how I saw my job. My job was to cheer people up. My job was to keep them from crying. If I could get a family through the funeral without tears, I thought I had done a masterful job.

I was forced to face my ignorance and I was determined to do something about it. That was in the early seventies so there were very few books available to read. I read all that I could find and the total was less than six. At that time I had never heard of such a thing as a self help group on any subject much less one dealing with grief. Without any guidance, I decided to gather a group of people who had recently suffered a death and begin what must be one of the earliest grief groups ever formed. All I knew to do was listen. Listening proved to be all these folks needed and it proved to be the best way for me to become educated about the grieving process. After a few years of this I began to write books on the subject and have spent almost half of my life writing and speaking about grief.

The longer I am involved with grieving people, the longer I study the process and communicate with others who are also involved in studying the process of grief, the more convinced I am that the funeral is a vital tool in the process of grief. When I started this chapter I said I had a deepening sense of fear and sorrow over the loss of the funeral. That fear and sorrow comes from the fact that I think the funeral, done right, is vital to the healing of broken hearts.

That fear and sorrow has lead me to writing this book. I wish to speak as a grief counselor who is looking at the funeral strictly from that perspective and trying to relate what I see as a valuable tool in grieving.

CHAPTER 2
The Value of Safety

The hardest thing for a grieving person to find is a safe place to grieve. Somehow we have developed the idea that the best way to handle grief is to not grieve. If we keep it under control people will complement us about how well we are doing, and how brave we are. The best thing we can possibly do with our grief is grieve. We are doing a good job with grief when we are crying our eyes out and making the whole world nervous in the process. Grief is not an enemy to be avoided, it is a process that leads to healing.

That concept of grief seems to run contrary to our very makeup. As soon as someone starts to cry we automatically begin trying to get them to stop. Not only are we convinced that tears are hard on people, we are also very uncomfortable when they are present. Most of us feel compelled to try to say words that will make the hurt go away. We begin explaining new ways to look at the loss. To show how much worse it could have been. To remind the person how much better off the loved one is now. To make up things to say about why God allowed this to happen.

The normal pattern we follow is first to explain: "You know the person is better off now. It's a blessing that your loved one is not suffering." If explanations do not work, we then try to argue: "Now you cannot let yourself think that way. You must get hold of yourself. You need to think of the good times and not dwell on the bad." If that doesn't work, we tend to criticize: "You are not *trying* to get well. You are just wallowing in your grief. It is time to put the past behind you and get on with your life." We do this with the best of intentions. We want to help and we are uncomfortable. That combination leads us to try to control and guide folks away from grieving in front of us.

People in grief are sensitive to our fears. It does not take but a moment for them to realize who is safe and who is not. If they sense our discomfort, they clam up and we lose a great chance to serve.

The funeral has traditionally been the one place where it is safe to grieve in public. The funeral home has always been a place of safety. It was all right to grieve there. It was all right to not be in control. The funeral director would understand because he or she deals with this all of the time. We have been gradually losing this sense of safety. As the funeral director has become more and more a professional funeral arranger and less and less the friend in need, people have learned to be more in control when in their presence.

The truth is, funeral directors are about as uncomfortable around tears as anyone else. That was one of the more shocking things I have learned in my life. When we began to write our aftercare program for funeral homes to use, we suggested that the funeral director send a personal note with the books when each was mailed. The first thing we heard was a desperate request for us to write the notes for them. They did not know what to say to grieving people.

When we were building the funeral home where I once was a partner, the funeral director and I had a rather long discussion about the furnishing for the arrangements room. He wanted a large desk. I thought the setting should be much less formal. Finally he became quite forceful and said, "We lose control of the family when we deal with them in such a relaxed setting. A desk helps keep them in control." I did not need to ask him what he meant by control. He did not want a family "losing it" in his presence. Unfortunately, we were not building a safe place.

I overheard a funeral director brag to another one that he could make the funeral arrangements in thirty minutes. I wanted to cry. One of the great values the funeral home offers to families is warm and safe people who do not need them to be in control. To force a family into an orchestrated plan of answering set questions is to rob them of one of our greatest gifts.

I fear the clergy are equally at fault. We fill the air with platitudes and scriptures that are designed to make it improper for the family to grieve in our presence. Realizing what my discomfort was doing to people led me into the study of grief. I would do almost anything to keep people from crying in my presence. I did not know what to say. I was afraid they would get out of control and I had no idea how to help them. I lived in fear and it showed. I was not raised in that kind of intimacy. I was not accustomed to sharing my own feelings and certainly was not comfortable with anyone else's.

My funeral messages basically said, "There is no reason to grieve. All is well. Heaven is real. So we should not be sad." My opening remarks at the funeral of a woman who was murdered by her husband was something like, "We are here to celebrate a victory." What I was really saying is, "Please don't be sad! I don't know what to do with sad people."

After the funeral, I would never mention the death again. If I was with a member of the family, I tried to be as upbeat as possible so they would be encouraged and happy. I thought cheering them up was the way to help them with their grieving.

We design funerals with keeping the family under control in mind. A large number of funeral homes sit the family off in a room so the rest of the audience will not have to see them cry, and so the family will not be embarrassed by their shedding of tears. This serves as a buffer for the family. They tend to tear up when they see their friends, so we place them where they cannot see or be seen.

When I suggested some new ideas in music for funerals, the first response I received was, "Won't that make the family cry?" I said, "It will if we are lucky."

If one of the great things the funeral has to offer to a family is a safe place to grieve, we need an atmosphere that welcomes the family to do so. The funeral home, the funeral director, and the funeral itself needs to be so warm and open that people will know this is a place of safety. This is the place where you can cry as long and as loud as you need to.

I tell people in grief that they need to "keep their cussing current". I do explain that I am using two words here. Cursing is using foul or bad language. Cussing is expressing feelings of sadness, loss and anger. We need to keep those feelings expressed, so we need to keep our cussing current. The funeral home should be a place where people automatically know it is all right to cuss.

CHAPTER 3
The Value of Participation

When my father-in-law died, my wife and her mother were several states away on a trip. I was called very early in the morning and soon found myself in a whirlwind of activity trying to get the two of them home, calling the funeral home, trying to figure out who should be called, and traveling to his home two hundred miles away.

After I arrived, it did not get much better. The phone was ringing constantly asking for information I did not have. People were arriving at the door with food and there was no one there to feed or comfort except me.

The next day when my wife and her mother were safely back, things got a little calmer. We went to the funeral home to make the arrangements. We were greeted by a very nice young man who showed us dignity and concern. We picked out the casket we thought best fit my father-in-law. We made all the other arrangements that go with planning a funeral. We decided who should officiate, who should sing and selected the songs. Later that day I took the necessary clothing to the funeral home.

That night I started a commuter service for the family. The funeral home was about thirty-five miles away and I was the one chosen to drive each family member as they arrived. On the day of the funeral I had duties too numerous to number. All of this was tiring. However, none of this was hard to do nor hard on me.

When my father died my schedule was even busier. He died in Texas where we lived so we had services there and in Oklahoma where he had lived for so many years. As my father approached his death we began having a series of talks about his funeral. We had to get past the "Just put me in a pine box and throw me in some ditch" stage that all men seem to feel the need to go through. Finally I told him the funeral was my gift to him and, if he did not mind, I would decide what kind of gift I would give him. He was pleased and relieved. From that day on, we had to go through the funeral step-by-step every time I was with him. He wanted to know who would speak, who would sing, who would be pall bearers, and every other detail imaginable. He had purchased cemetery lots in Oklahoma and wanted to be sure he would be buried there. He did not like Texas much.

When he died, I had the privilege of helping pick out his casket. We took our time and chose with great care. This was our dad and we wanted things to be right. We chose the casket piece from the florist. We selected the songs with the same care. He loved the old hymns and it was difficult to decide which ones he loved the most. We planned both of the services with great care and felt the whole process was an act of love. The participation had great meaning for us. It was not just something to "keep us occupied so we would not dwell on his death." It was a vital part of our healing. We were able to express our love in a tangible way, and it felt good.

I did not know the meaning of this involvement until my mother-in-law died. She was living in Texas so we could take care of her. We called the same funeral home that had served her husband. The funeral director asked if we wanted the same casket as the one we used for her husband. We said that would be fine. We were able to take care of the rest of the details by long distance and were through in a very short time. She died early in the morning on December 31 which happened to fall on a weekend that year. We knew we could not have the funeral until Monday, but we found out there was a large wedding at the church on that day so the funeral had to be moved to Tuesday. We spent Saturday, Sunday, and Monday in our home in Texas biding our time with no involvement in the funeral except some phone calls.

Tuesday morning we drove to Oklahoma. We arrived at the church in time for a lunch served by the church members. We sat in a parlor and greeted many of my mother-in-law's friends. Then we went upstairs for the funeral. I was very close to my mother-in-law. You never hear mother-in-law jokes from me. She was one of the happiest ladies I ever knew and she loved me as well. She loved to say that behind every successful man stands a surprised mother-in-law. Even though I loved her husband very much, I was much closer to her than I was to him. Her funeral was almost meaningless to me. I did not shed a tear. It seemed like we were at a funeral for someone else's loved one. We were not a part of the process. It was a function put on by someone else. We were just onlookers at the event. When participation is not there, the funeral doesn't mean as much.

That has meaning for funeral service as we try to lead people to purchase pre-need funeral plans. I believe in the financial part of pre-need and think every family should take care of that part. But I have great problems with totally planning a funeral. The family needs involvement. The participation is not hard on them, it is part of the healing a funeral can offer to families. It is counterproductive for us to present pre-need as a way to save families from having to make these tough decisions at this time. These are not tough decisions, and they are not hard on families. This kind of presentation leads folks to think if funerals are so hard on families maybe we should not have one, or, if we do, we should have a minimal service at best. This helps establish the idea that immediate disposition is much easier on the family.

We are hearing more and more about the need to "personalize" the funeral. Most of the time that means things like picture boards and other mementoes at the funeral. Personalization, as you will hear many times in this book, is more than pictures. Personalization also means allowing the family to participate in the whole process in whatever degree they desire and are comfortable doing. Take away participation and the picture boards don't mean much.

Participation is a way of showing love. We will discover in a later chapter that people need to establish the significance of their loved one. The participation is a wonderful way to begin this process. Picking out just the right casket brings to mind how much love was there. Carefully planning the service leads to examining what the relationship meant.

Participation helps us face reality. As we involve ourselves in the process, the death becomes real. That may sound harsh and hard on the family, but the reality turns our grieving loose and releases our feelings. It is the first step toward healing.

Participation draws the family into the process. Families will usually build barriers between each other and try to act stronger than they are. I don't want to tell my brother how much I hurt until I know how much he hurts, so I say nothing. The participation will usually break down these barriers and the family will begin grieving in front of one another.

Of course there will be those times when the family will not agree and there may even be arguments over the choices. That is not all bad. Most of the time the choices are not the issue, they are just safe things to argue about and release some tensions. The only time my mother's family ever fought was during the funeral process for my grandmother. They cleared the air and it was healthy.

It is not only important to say that participation should happen. It is also important to realize there is no

other way to offer participation to a family except through the funeral. When there is no funeral, all of the benefits of participation are not available.

CHAPTER 4

The Value of Symbols and Ceremony

When someone suggests to me that funerals are not important and have very little value to the family, I always answer by saying, "Can you imagine the impact on our nation if President Kennedy had been immediately cremated and his body buried in secrecy? Or can you imagine England not having a state funeral when Princess Diana died?"

In both cases, whole nations found healing in the symbols and ceremonies of a funeral. Thousands passed by the body of the President as he lay in state under the Capital rotunda. It mattered that he lay on the catafalque used for the body of President Lincoln. The symbol of both the rotunda and the catafalque were not lost on any of us.

The family and dignitaries dressed in morning coats while taking the slow walk to the church and then to the gravesite is still vivid in our minds. The caisson that carried his body, the riderless horse, the band playing music that stirred our pride and tears at the same time. The lighting of the eternal flame was a fitting symbol that brought a sense of closure to the service. The flame gave an assurance that life will last past this life, and that he would never be forgotten.

The same was true for Princess Diana. London was stacked knee deep in flowers, each petal being a symbol of love and pain. The slow walk by her children so they could feel the outpouring of love from the people lining the way. The carrying of her body into the church. The church itself with more history than even its massive walls could contain. A song we will never forget sung by a friend.

How could either nation face the tragedy and loss without seeing these symbols and experiencing these ceremonies?

I have seen the meaning in the faces of families as airplanes flew by and preformed the missing man maneuver. I am always moved to tears and I never was in the military nor have I been a pilot.

Our ceremonies are not as grand nor as dramatic as these, but they have the same meaning and the same importance. When words fail, ceremony takes over.

I have watched countless Masonic rituals and, since I am not a Mason, I did not find much meaning there but a glimpse at a widow hearing the ceremonies her husband loved and followed let me know I was in the presence of something meaningful.

Since I am not a Catholic, I do not understand how precious the ceremonies followed every Sunday of a lifetime can become when there is a death in the family. I have watched in awe.

I have seen ceremonies that were so personal in nature that no one in the audience even noticed or understood, but the family found wonderful meaning.

A lovely voice sang *Red Sails In The Sunset* at the funeral of my good friend's wife. No one knew that was the song they danced to the night they wed. But the family knew, and ten years later they still talk about what that song meant.

In our efforts to act like no one has died and make it all go away as quickly as possible, we forfeit these wonderfully meaningful expressions of love. Expressions that have meaning now and offer healing memories in the months to come.

One of the more dramatic illustrations of the power of symbols came from a rescue worker in the Oklahoma City Bombing. When he returned home he wrote about his experience and I had the good fortune to read it. I do not have his exact words but they were something like,

> *Every time we came up out of that hell hole we would see the families gathered near the fence that kept them out of the area. They always gathered at the corner nearest the building aching to be as much a part of the rescue effort as possible. We always had the urge to go to the wall, give them a hug, and just talk with them. This was not possible because we were contaminated and had to go through decontamination. We were discouraged from any contact because of the emotional impact it would have on us. We also had to conserve every ounce of our energy. Someone came up with the plan for us to make one Teddy Bear our designated hugger. As soon as we finished decontamination we would give*

the bear a hug. At designated times each day that bear was taken to the fence for the families to hug. Somehow that simple ceremony took on great meaning for all of us. We felt connected to those families and knew the bear was telling them how much we loved them and hurt with them.

Never underestimate the power of symbols and ceremonies. In that simple ceremony, both the families and the workers found connection and love.

CHAPTER 5

The Value of Reality and Closure

I became a believer in the value of a family viewing the body of a loved one long before I started writing about grief. As a pastor I tried to be with the family the first time they saw their loved one. I expected this to be the hardest part of the funeral and thought that was the time for me to be there to support. I saw this as a terrible ordeal for a family to endure. Over time it became more and more clear to me that this was not an ordeal. On the contrary, families find great meaning and peace in this experience.

I saw them gaze lovingly as if they were drinking in the picture that was to last for the rest of their lives. They would touch the hair, pat the hands, and talk to one another about how peaceful the person looked.

Many families had been through a long illness and had watched their loved one's body become almost unrecognizable. Now they had a chance to see the person as they were before the illness took such a toll. I hear people say they want to remember the person as they were. That is fine as long as we don't have to see them while they are ill. I stood with my father while he died. I cannot express how grateful I am that what I saw that day is not my last vision of my father.

Embalming is an art whose value cannot be measured. It is my hope that we will never diminish that value. I sense the need for a renewal of our commitment to present loved ones with great skill and care. We not only present a loving last look, we present a valuable part of the healing process.

A widow whose husband died in a car crash said, "It just isn't real until you see it, is it?" It is natural to think that this reality is much harder on a family and they should avoid this shock and pain. The reality hurts, but until there is reality there can be no progress with the grieving process. As in most things in life, the easy way can become the hardest in the long run.

I had a friend whose son was killed in a plane crash that took the lives of an entire football team. All he had left were the ashes the airline sent to him. He told me how difficult it was to believe that his son was gone. He had visions that somehow his son had survived and was lost in the mountains where the plane crashed. He hired airplanes to fly over the area looking for his son. The fact that the plane was totally destroyed and no one could have survived did not mean anything to him. He said he could not get past the disbelief and the need to search until he did something he was not suppose to do. He happened to be a funeral director so he knew he could look through the ashes and find his son's teeth. He had them examined to prove to himself that this was actually his son.

One of the toughest deaths I ever had to help a family face was a member of my church who was murdered in a motel room. His head was virtually destroyed with a pipe wrench. We made the decision that the family should not view his body. If I had known then what I know now I think we would have shown the family what we could and covered the rest. A wife and two children had said good-bye one morning and never saw him again. They had to take the word of others who said that the body they found in the motel room was his. Over the years I watched as they struggled to find reality and closure. I think it was especially hard on the children.

Trauma like this does not just go away. Just because the children learned to act like they were fine and put on a good front does not mean the impact of this kind of event will just go away. We have no way of knowing how many cases of substance abuse, eating disorders, and angry rebellion start with traumas that are not faced and are left to fester until they come out in some destructive manner.

There needs to be some method for reality and the beginning of closure. Closure has become a bad word for those in grief. They respond quite vociferously that there is no such thing. They are right. There are many experiences of closure and I am not sure the experience is ever finished. If closure is a process, this is the beginning of that process.

My experiences convinced me that viewing the body was important, but I had no idea how important until the son of my former office manager died of suicide.

He was only sixteen when he put a gun to his head and pulled the trigger. I happened to be in town that day and when the call came I followed his mother to the house. I arrived just as she was headed into the room where Justin lay. I stopped her, and she protested that she wanted to see him. I suggested that she see him that night. She insisted that she did not want to see him in a casket and I assured her he would be on a bed, so she relented and did not go into the room.

The funeral director performed miracles that day, and that night I went with the mother, father and two sisters to see Justin. I am still grateful that we had that time of closure. Those who complain about the high cost of funerals should experience something like that night. I have no idea what that funeral cost, I do know that one night was worth every penny.

About a year later, the mother told me she was going to do something that she was not sure I would agree with. She was going to the police and get the pictures they took of Justin in the room where he died. I began to respond and she said, "I know those pictures are going to hurt. I know they are bad. You did a good job of cleaning up, but I found evidence for weeks after he died. I have spent a year hearing people whisper that he blew his head off. Those pictures cannot possibly be as bad as my imagination has made it. I have to know."

She got the pictures. We looked at them together. I waited a few months and then asked her what seeing those pictures had meant to her. She said, "I can't tell you what a relief the pictures have been. They are so much better than my imagination had made it."

I told that story to a group of mothers who had also lost children to suicide. One jumped up and shouted, "There will be pictures!" I said "Yes, there will be pictures." I thought she was going to start home that night if she had to walk all the way. She could not wait to get the pictures of her son. She wrote me later and said she had gotten the pictures. She was afraid to look at them by herself so she had her counselor look with her. She said the pictures were a source of great comfort. They were so much better than her imagination had made it.

In our efforts to protect people, we leave it to their imaginations. I am convinced that imagination will inevitably make it worse. Every time we protect people from reality, we seem to end up hurting instead of helping.

I can't help but think of the children. For generations we have tried to protect them from the awful experiences of the funeral. They are shuffled off somewhere else during the funeral. I hear people say the funeral would be too hard on them. They are not allowed to say good-bye to loved grandparents because the experience might traumatize them. In our efforts to protect, we leave it to their imaginations. That which is left to the imagination is an invitation to nightmares and struggle.

The truth is, after years of trying to help people walk through their grief, I know of nothing that helps give reality to the experience as much as the family viewing the body of the loved one. That is a true value.

CHAPTER 6

The Value of Significance

I discovered a word that has gradually consumed me from a young woman who had suffered the death of a husband while she was very young. After her remarriage she had also lost a child. She was explaining the difference in the grief following the loss of a mate and that following the loss of a child. She said, "The grief of losing a mate is a process of turning loose, of saying good-bye. The grief following the death of a child is a process of hanging on, of trying not to say good-bye. You feel like the child did not live long enough to establish his or her significance and so you must establish it for them. That is why grieving parents want someone to call the child's name. We want to be sure the child is remembered."

The word, "significance" stuck in my mind. The more I thought about that word the larger it became. So large that my daughters tease me by saying that I only know three words and I have written twenty-five books about those three words. I sound like a broken record and end up saying the same thing over and over, but the idea of significance grows larger and larger in the grieving process.

When things happen to us, the first thing we want and need to do is establish the significance of that event. No matter what the event is. If something wonderful happens we feel like we will explode if we can't find someone to tell. We may seem to be bragging and bore our friends to distraction, but we must share the good news.

The same is true when bad things happen. A woman got on the airport commuter bus the other day and announced to the whole bus that she hoped the plane was on time because she was on her way to her mother's funeral. No one responded but she felt much better because everyone on board knew what she was going through. That was not a search for sympathy. That was the natural response we all have to the things that cause us pain. We need to tell someone.

If we can establish significance we can move on. If we cannot do so we tend to stop progressing and the hurt can become an obsession to us.

My grandson was crying one day and complaining that his cousin had hit him. The normal parental reaction would be to say, "Stop being a tattletale and you kids play nice or I will come in there and you will be sorry." Instead of that reaction I knelt down so we could be face to face and said, "I am sorry that happened to you." He said, "Do you want to go play catch?" All he needed was for someone to understand the significance of what happened to him. What works with small children, works with adults as well.

I met two sisters who said their mother was the most negative person they had ever known. She remembered every hurt that had ever happened to her. Negative had become the automatic response to every thing that happened. I asked them what was the thing their mother said the most often. They said, "The thing she says the most, and the thing that hurts us the deepest is, that her life stopped the day her little boy died. She still has us and our brother died sixty-one years ago." I said, "I wish you would try something. It may not work but the next time she says that, reach over and touch her and ask her how that made her feel." Most likely when her son died no one let her establish the significance of her son or the loss and, sixty-one years later, she is still trying to get that significance established.

If we cannot establish significance we tend to develop an obsession about the event in question. Twenty years or sixty years later we can still be trying to get someone to understand our loss. A hurt that will not go away or a grudge that is carried for years are not there because someone is too hardheaded to forgive or too weak to recover. They are there because no one allowed the person the right to establish the significance of that event and over time this need became an obsession. Collect enough obsessions and the basic element of a personality becomes negative.

The hardest part of grieving is finding a way to establish this significance. Friends and family are not comfortable with people talking about their pain. They are not comfortable with people talking about the person who has died. They want to jump in and move the conversation to happier things. The opposite of significance is trivialization. We trivialize when we try to explain it away. We trivialize when we try to put the best face on it. We trivialize when we try to force someone to move on in their grief.

Trivialization always makes the person in grief angry. No matter what is used in the trivialization process, it makes the person angry. I have been meeting with a family whose daughter was killed by a drunk driver six days before she was to be married. I meet with the girl's mother, brother and sister, and her fiancé on a somewhat regular basis. The father was also killed by a drunk driver six years earlier. The mother said, "Your book was the only one I would read when my husband died. The scriptures in the others made me angry." I found that to be almost shocking. Her husband was a minister and she and the children are still very active in their faith.

The problem was the scriptures the other books used were the ones that trivialized her grief at the time when she was trying to establish the depth and breadth of her pain. There are many scriptures that heal, but the ones we tend to use and the ones we are most comfortable with, are the ones that try to explain the grief away. We can tell someone who is twenty years down the road from a death that "All things work together for good," but if we do that the next day after a death they will probably want us to leave. When we say "God will not put more on us than we can bear," we are intimating that the death is not an unbearable burden right at the time when they are trying to let the world know just how unbearable the burden is.

The urge to trivialize is almost overwhelming. Somehow we have this tremendous need to explain things so the hurt will go away. In the process we can say some terrible things to people. I am working with a woman whose daughter was murdered. Someone has already tried to force her to see that her daughter was headed down the wrong path and it was probably a blessing that she was taken before things got too bad. When I hear those kinds of things, I shudder.

When a person is lost there are two levels of significance. First we need to establish the significance of the person and of our loss. It is almost as if we must inventory the loss before we can grieve it. We don't know what we have lost until it is gone. After a person dies there is a period of time when we are discovering something new to miss on an almost hourly basis. Something we want to ask them. Something we want to share with them. Things we will no longer have because they are not there. The things we will miss the most. Some people call that wallowing in grief, and I say, "Yes, and they should wallow on." This is the process of healing grief.

This process demands that we talk about the person. We may glorify them beyond recognition of course, but it doesn't matter. There will be plenty of time for a more realistic look later. For now we need to have the freedom to inventory our loss. I think this is the missing link in the grieving process.

Then we need to establish the social significance. We need to know how much our loved one meant to others. *That is why we have funerals.* A funeral is a time for folks to gather and share with us the fact that they, too, loved our loved one. That they, too, have suffered a loss. Nothing feels better to a person than this discovery. "Someone else thought my loved one was significant."

Into this need comes the funeral. There is no better place or no better way to establish the significance of a person than a healthy, well-done funeral. To miss this is to miss the best chance we have. The whole process is aimed at significance, from the choosing of a casket, through the planning of a funeral, to the funeral itself. The whole of the funeral is aimed at significance. I have a button I wish I could give to every funeral director and every minister. The button says, "I sell significance."

Significance is all I want to buy. I don't want a casket. I need one, but I don't want one. I don't want a funeral sermon. I need one, but I don't want one. I don't want to be hauled around in a nice family car. That is convenient at a time of need, but I don't want it. What I want and what I need is to establish the significance of the person I have lost and the depths of my pain.

It goes without saying that while the funeral is the major source for this significance, not all funerals fit this need. A cookie cutter funeral that is not personalized to the loved one, not only does not establish significance it also trivializes. This kind of funeral says the person is not important enough for us to take the time necessary to memorialize his or her life. When a funeral is done and the person's name has not even been spoken, the family has been trivialized. Period.

We hold in our hands a valuable tool for helping people at the time of their greatest need. We must treasure this opportunity as the ministry of our lives.

SECTION II
THE CHALLENGES

CHAPTER 7
The Dilemma

Everything I have said so far is known almost by instinct. We instinctively know the value of reality and having a time of saying good-bye. Just looking at how desperately we search for bodies after a disaster reveals how much value we place on this process. Feeling the pain of those families who still wait to hear from a loved one who is missing in action from the Vietnam War, is more than enough to prove the point.

A few days after the Oklahoma City bombing I was called on to write some special words for those families who the rescuers felt would not receive a body. At the time they thought as high as fifty bodies would not be found and it was readily apparent that this would compound their loss. I wrote the words so they could also be given to those who were not allowed to view the bodies that were found. I knew their lack of viewing would compound the loss.

If bodies do not matter, why do we turn heaven and earth to find every possible part of those lost in an air disaster? I have talked with funeral directors who gave massive numbers of hours in the identification and care of these victims. There is nothing too hard nor too expensive when it comes to finding these bodies.

We spent millions of dollars trying to find John Kennedy Jr., his wife and her sister, then we put them right back where we found them. I have not heard one person question this rather strange action. If the family is not helped by the process then why not just identify the plane, assume that the three bodies were the victims, have a brief service on shore and let it go at that? To even suggest such a thing is unthinkable.

If times of memorialization don't matter, why do we build monuments on shore when planes crash at sea? I recently visited Peggy's Cove in Nova Scotia. That is the sight of the Swiss Air Crash. A large monument stands vigil and there is a constant stream of visitors who come and pay homage. I do not know any of those victims, but it had meaning to me to stand there and look out toward the place were the plane fell.

The fact is, bodies and memorials do matter and we know that they do. This brings me face-to-face with a dilemma I cannot fathom. I cannot understand how these truths can be so self evident, and there be a massive movement away from the traditional funeral at the same time.

Finding answers to that dilemma is, of course, the number one priority to funeral service. It does not take a genius to know that funeral service is facing serious difficulties, and that if solutions are not found we may lose the funeral as we know it.

If over forty percent of the customers in a restaurant decided they were just going to have coffee from now on and not eat the food, we would conclude that the restaurant was in trouble. If forty percent of those customers said they weren't even going to drink the coffee, we might think that place is not long for this world. In many parts of the United States and Canada, those are the very figures we face.

Finding answers should also be high on the priority list for the clergy. I was asked to write an article for a magazine published by the Southern Baptist. The editor said he wanted an article that would explain the importance of the funeral to the clergy. I tried to explain the values of the funeral in much the same way as I have done in this book.

I added to that list the chance to be relevant in the lives of people. We not only become irrelevant when we fail to talk in the language of the people. We also become irrelevant when people have to go outside the church to find help when they hurt. If we do not learn how to make the funeral a meaningful experience of healing for the people we serve, they will be forced to find help outside of the church. That is the ultimate irrelevance.

There is also a social significance involved. A nation that does not honor its dead will ultimately lose its reverence for life. If the dead do not matter, it will not be long until the living don't matter either.

Since we have never had to face this issue it is hard for us to grasp how important a sense of connectedness to our roots can be. When Hitler took over Poland, he destroyed their cemeteries. He wanted to take away all connection with their heritage. I heard a woman tell how she thought all of her ancestors graves had been lost. She felt a terrible sense of loneliness that could not be filled. She made a trip to Poland and found one cemetery the Germans had missed. She had a distant grandfather buried there. She wept as she told what that discovery meant and still means to her. We need to explore the long term impact of cremation and scattering to the wind. Future generations may well feel the same sense of loss felt by that woman.

My dilemma is–since we understand the need, why are more and more people choosing to have less and less in the way of a funeral? Why is it open season for articles blasting the funeral and the funeral directors as too costly and even hinting that the whole process is a rip-off? More intriguing to me is why is no one challenging these articles and defending the practice?

The usual answer to these questions is that funerals are too costly. I asked the audience at every conference of funeral directors why they think people are moving away from the traditional funeral and cost is always listed as the number one reason. I think that is wrong.

The problem is not the cost. The problem is that people do not see the value of the funeral. If they saw value, the cost would not be much of an issue. I think that can be proven with one simple comparison. The average cost of a funeral at this time is between $5,000.00 and $8,000.00, depending on the locality. The average cost of a wedding is about $20,000.00. No one is writing articles about the high cost of marriage. There are no exposé about florists ripping people off at this most vulnerable of times. Why? Because people see value in weddings and they do not see value in funerals.

They do not see value in funerals because no one tells them. Too often even the funeral director does not know the value or how to talk about the meaning. I am sorry to say that the clergy are also uninformed and often they can be the leading spokespersons for the anti-funeral camp.

The funeral service industry itself has not done a very good job of telling our story. We have a story to tell, but we stand mute before the world. We have no national voice speaking for us or defending us. We think if we speak up we come across as self-serving and so we stand mute. Every other profession can toot their horns till the cows come home, but we must stand in silence. People will never know the value of the funeral until we learn how to tell them.

I wrote a small funeral planner for people who are going to have their loved one cremated. I did so because it is apparent that people do not know the options that are available to them. They do not know that the family can view the body and still use cremation as the final disposition. I found out that if they knew the options, many would chose to view, and since I think that is important, I wrote a book that tells them about these options.

I was in a large funeral home recently and these books were on the table in the arrangement room. The funeral director said, "When I read this book, I became curious about the other books in my library. I have a large library and I read through all of them. This is the only book in this place that tells a family about the importance of viewing a body. The only one." I was flattered and angry at the same time. There should be hundreds of books telling our story. People are not going to know the value if we don't tell them. We dare not presume and I fear a great deal of our problems stem from many years of just presuming about the people we serve.

Part of this problem stems from the difficulty in telling the value of the funeral without seeming to be self-serving. When we speak of the value we can just hear people saying, "What else would you expect to hear? They are just trying to sell me a funeral." This feeling has left us tongue tied and silent. No one talks about the funeral.

We don't have to talk about the funeral. Anytime we talk about the grief process we say the things that make the funeral matter. We need to train some people to impact our communities with helps for the grieving. It is simple and natural to talk about the need to establish the significance. The idea of a meaningful funeral is implied.

Chapter 8

The Challenge of a Scattered Society

We don't live where we once did. In former times if there were six children in a family, five of them would live in the general area of their births. One would get away, and we would talk about them as if they thought they were too good for the rest of the family and had to move off to get away. Now all six of the children are gone. One of the growing economic issues is the cost to industry in time and productivity caused by employees trying to care for aging loved ones who live hundreds or thousands of miles away. There is no longer a core group of family living in the old home towns.

When I was a child I thought I was related to most of the town where I lived. By the time my father died, I did not have even a distant cousin living in my home town. We buried my father in a strange land because we had no one back home to visit his grave. We live in a scattered society and this scattering has had some profound effects on the funeral.

The Old Loyalties are No Longer There

There was a time when a funeral home knew the families it served. Certain families almost belonged to a funeral home. Often the funeral director would refer to them as one of "our families." When a death happened in one of those families the funeral director got ready to have a funeral. It was unthinkable that that family would go anywhere else. The grandparents had been buried by that funeral home and the rest of the family would follow as a matter of course.

Then they all moved away. They no longer see the funeral director at Rotary club on Wednesdays. They soon forget about who was in charge of the last funeral. They do not know the current clergy person either. When a death occurs they come in from out of town and just put a service together without much thought as to who is in charge. They do not know how funerals are done in the area. They were young when they lived in the town and did not attend very many funerals. They do not know what is proper or possible in a funeral. All they know is they must return to bury a loved one and they must do so with total strangers.

My family belonged to one of the two funeral homes in our small town. When a family member died we did not ask who had the body, we just went to that home for visitation. After I moved away and the only contact I had with the town was an occasional trip there for a funeral, I did not even think about those old loyalties. We used a different funeral home for a very close relative and I did not even notice the change. The funeral director from the funeral home we always used is a friend of mine and he wrote me a very nice letter asking me to explain what he had done to hurt our feelings. I did not know how to answer him. He had not done anything except maybe he let us slip through his fingers by taking us for granted. He did not do anything to maintain the old loyalties and somehow they died.

The Scattering Creates Hassles for the Family

After I returned to my home town for the funerals of both of my parents, and to my wife's home town for the funerals of her parents I began to understand why immediate disposition or just a graveside service is becoming more and more attractive to families. Having a funeral in a distant city creates problems and hassles one must experience to believe.

A few months ago my wife and I attended the funeral of her uncle in a small town in Arizona. Unfortunately our trip is probably typical of what families experience in the trips back home to bury their dead. We arrived in the early evening the night before the funeral. Most of the family arrived at about the same time and without any planning we just met at the funeral home. The plans had already been made by the more immediate members of the family, at least by those who could get there in time. Since the family is scattered we did not know each other very well. In some cases we were trying to grieve with family members we had never met.

We had made our travel plans without any notice and with very little knowledge of motel availability or even where the funeral home was located. We flew into the nearest city and arrived by rental car for the funeral which was to happen the next morning.

We gathered at the funeral home and spent more time introducing ourselves to one another than we did in viewing the uncle or in talking about who he was and what he meant to us. We hurried through the viewing because the funeral director seemed to be anxious to close the funeral home. Fortunately, the uncle's house was still available for us to use after we finished the viewing. In many cases the loved ones have been living in nursing homes and the family home has been sold. These families have no place to gather for a time of grieving together. Motel lobbies are not very conducive to family grief sessions.

Then came the panic. We had so little time to prepare for the trip it had not dawned on us to arrange for flowers. My wife's brother and sister called and asked us to purchase a spray from the three families. We were in a small town with no knowledge of florists and the funeral was the next morning. I was on the doorstep of a florist when they opened the next morning, but florists don't open very early. Although it was late the florist agreed to make us a floral presentation and get it to the church on time.

After all of the hassle, the cost, and the travel we gathered in a small church for a cookie cutter funeral. The same songs, the same order of service, and the same old tired message from a pastor we did not know and who did not know us. I sat there wondering why people go to so much trouble, then it hit me, more and more of them aren't willing to go through this kind of thing for a service with no more meaning than the one we were sitting through. After a trip or so home, they decide to "Just do a graveside."

Many of these Scattered Families will be Buried in Your City

The hassles may not seem to be all that important, but many of these people will ultimately be buried in their home towns. As our society scatters the displacement leaves us with no where to go. My wife and I have struggled with our own burial place. We, like most of society, have moved from place to place until we do not have a "home town" of our own. We left our own homes so long ago that we no longer know very many people there and have no kinsmen there.

When my dad died we buried him in the city where we lived at that time. My parents had moved there to be near one of their children. Mother wanted Dad to be near her so we buried him there. After her death, we moved away from that city. Somehow it became important to me to have my folks in the city where they lived for over seventy years and where they were known. I moved their bodies there and bought cemetery lots for my wife and me at the same time.

Some day my family will face the hassles of going to a strange place to have a funeral. They will have no place to stay. There will be no place for the family to gather and visit. They will not know the funeral director nor the minister. They will simply be taking me home.

A scattered society presents some unique challenges to our industry. There must be some thought given to how we can reduce the hassles and make these experiences worth the time and trouble. We must find new ways to keep up with our families as they scatter, and we must find new ways to serve them when they return.

CHAPTER 9

The Challenge of an Outdated Product

People do not know the value of the funeral because far too often there is little value there. We have not kept the funeral on the cutting edge of change. I can plan the next fifty funerals for almost every funeral home and never leave my office to do so. They will follow the same patterns we have followed for years. I was a minister for thirty-seven years and still consider myself active in that work. The funeral today is exactly what the funeral was the first day I started in the ministry.

I recently conducted a funeral for a friend of mine. The funeral was in a distant city so I arrived just a few hours before the funeral was to begin. I had no worry about such a brief time to prepare since I knew the procedure by heart. There was no reason to even check in with the funeral home to see if there would be anything new happening or anything different in the service. I went to see the family and arrived at the funeral home about thirty minutes before the funeral was to start.

The funeral director greeted me by handing me the same obituary form I have seen for years. He directed me to the room reserved for the clergy to use until time for the service to begin. About ten minutes before the service was to begin the people doing the music arrived. The singer flipped through the hymnal to find the requested songs and after a second to glance through the verses, told the organist what he planned to do. No rehearsal, no thought. The person who was to assist me with the service arrived about the same time and asked me what scriptures he should read and what he should say. We put the whole thing together in less than fifteen minutes and the show went on.

I sat through the service thinking that my friend deserved better than this. He was one of the best men I have ever known. He gave his time to helping others in more ways than I can count. He had been a supporter to me when I needed his support. He was more important than a fifteen minute effort and a service just like all the other services I have experienced or even produced.

This kind of funeral no longer fits our society. We have become far too sophisticated to tolerate this for much longer. Every other facet of our lives features well-done presentations or they don't exist. No one can get by with sloppiness in a world accustomed to instant entertainment on television. Our society now looks for experiences that are moving and engaging. Anyone who is trying to get by with less will ultimately fail.

Even the church has had to notice and change. The running joke used to be that the seven last words of the church were "We've never done it this way before." Many churches have changed their whole approach to the worship service. Orchestras have replaced organ music. There are guitars everywhere you look. The only place on earth where church sopranos still stand beside a Hammond organ to sing is in the funeral home. The churches who have resisted these changes are watching their members flock to the churches who offer the experiences they are seeking.

I may not like all of the changes. I would love to hear someone dare sing without a tape backup by the London Philharmonic Orchestra, but that is me and I am a little old fashioned. I miss the hymns of my youth. The praise choruses of today sound like two notes, two words, sung for two hours. But when I look at the young couples and the young people in the pews, I sing along. At least the words are easy for even someone as old as me to remember.

Then I go to the next funeral. Same song, second verse. Same order of service. The only change is whether or not the minister will end in prayer. Same droning on of platitudes. And we wonder why folks don't think they are getting their money's worth?

At a recent funeral a family wanted the country song *Daddy's Hands* played from a CD by the artist that recorded the song. We worked it into the service and it was a beautiful experience of personalization for the father. Someone who was at that service and heard the song, had a loved one die a week or so later. They wanted *Daddy's Hands* at their funeral. No one guided them. They said they wanted the song, and someone asked them who they wanted to sing it. They said the lady that directs the choir at their church would be fine.

Daddy's Hands was not designed to be played on a piano. Nor was it written to be sung by a church soprano. The pianist and the singer practiced as best they could and arrived at the funeral home the usual ten minutes before the service. To their horror they found there was no piano in the funeral home. They had to do it on the Hammond organ. When the time came for the song they also found out they did not know how to turn on the organ. The funeral director finally arrived after a long and awkward time of silence, and he did not know how to turn it on either. Somehow they finally got it going and I wish they had not been able to do so. It was awful. I can't tell you how awful it really was because my wife was the one playing the organ.

The funeral director thought nothing of what happened. He had delivered "What the family asked for," so his job was done. Somehow we must learn how to never let that happen. Somehow we must learn how to produce a better product than that and still let the family make the decisions. We must learn how to guide without taking over. We must have better funerals.

CHAPTER 10
A Challenge to the Clergy

I am afraid I must admit that some of the problem with the funeral must be lain at the feet of my chosen profession. The clergy has not discovered the value or the power of the funeral. Far too often the funeral is an unpleasant chore we must do. A chore that interrupts every vacation of our lives and inevitably comes at the wrong time the rest of the year. It is an unpleasant task, which we are not well prepared to perform. Our training does not properly prepare us to deal with grieving people. Most of us feel a cold chill at the prospect of trying to figure out what to say to a mother whose child has just died. We are expected to know exactly what to say in such cases, but too often we are expected to do so with absolutely no training or experience at all.

It has always amazed me at how much knowledge the clergy are suppose to just have. I declared my intentions to enter the ministry as a high school senior. The next day, grown people were asking my advice about the Bible. Great knowledge was suppose to come with the call. I have spent most of my life bluffing my way through demands that made my insides churn violently.

I remember talking with a woman on an airplane. When she found out I was to speak to a clergy conference on grief she said, "Well don't they already know all about that sort of thing?"

We are also not taught in the art or meaning of the funeral. The first funeral I ever attended as an adult was one at which I officiated. I had no idea what happened nor when it was to happen. Fortunately, I was to be assisted by an elderly pastor who was kind enough to know that I needed help without showing that he knew how ignorant I was.

In most seminaries today, there still is very little emphasis or teaching about the funeral. There may be some comments in pastoral care class, but the study of theology leaves very little time for such mundane things as how to conduct funerals or weddings.

There is also very little taught about grieving or how to help people through their grief. When I started writing about grief I assumed that one of the best markets for my writings would be the church. I thought there would be a deep hunger for knowledge about helping our people walk through their pain. One of the great shocks of my life was learning how wrong I was. I have been writing and speaking on the subject for almost twenty-five years and the first indication of interest from the church has happened in the last five years. There seems to be a growing interest now, but it has been a long time coming.

This interest has come in just the nick of time. A Gallop poll taken in December 1997 revealed that "many Americans long for spiritual support as they reach the end of their lives, but few say they would choose clergy to provide it." The survey went on to say that "50 percent said they consider prayer important at life's end, and 44 percent said they would like to receive spiritual counseling at that time, but only 36 percent said they would call on a clergy person to give this comfort." That is frightening to me. If we lose folks in this area we have lost them for good. We must learn everything we can about helping people in their grief. The best way to share this knowledge and our concern is to present a meaningful and healing funeral.

The problem with the funeral is made worse by the dilemma the funeral presents to the clergy person. Many are torn between the chance to evangelize the living or honoring the dead. Some of my best friends in the ministry feel they must either seek to evangelize or they have denied their faith. This seems to be an opportunity that cannot be passed by without guilt.

Since I came from that background and have felt those feelings I had to struggle to an answer for myself. I don't know what is right for anyone else, I just know what I decided was right for me. I saw the funeral as a chance to give "cups of cold water in His name." I decided that I had a much better chance to reach a family by ministering to them in their pain, than I did by preaching at them during the service. I studied the grieving process and decided the best thing I could do was to help them establish the significance of the person and the loss. I must say that I have never met anyone who told me they were converted at a funeral. I can show many families that were reached because the funeral was made meaningful to their needs.

Other clergy persons are torn between worship and eulogy. Many come from backgrounds and are deeply embedded in the meaning of the ceremonies of worship. To them, the funeral is a worship service. Some of them feel the eulogizing of the person takes away from the worship of God. I will never forget talking to an elderly priest whose bishop had ordered his priests to emphasize the eulogy. This fine man wanted to follow his bishop but, to him, such actions would have been blasphemy.

So here the clergy person stands, with no training and no models, with the funeral experience resting on their shoulders. The funeral director does not want to interfere with either the clergy person's plans nor those of the family, so they are not going to give any guidance. The clergy are novices at best and have very little idea what a funeral should be. It is no wonder we are producing some very bad funerals.

The easy way out so far has been to develop, at most, two messages and just repeat them over and over. The names change to protect our reputations but the message is the same. I have heard funeral directors laugh about how they know exactly when to get ready for the ending of the service. They have heard the same words hundreds of times.

I have also heard families express great distress because the clergy person did not even call the loved one's name. Recently a mother told me that the clergy person who conducted the funeral for her young daughter did not know she was the girl's mother until after the funeral.

When I started going around the country talking to people in grief I was amazed at how much anger grieving people have toward the clergy. I hear it at almost every conference. They feel let down and rejected. They are mad because the funeral was so impersonal. Impersonal funerals trivialize the life. Far too often they are angry at the church as well. Since the church does not know much about grief, they don't know the importance of walking with the family after the funeral. Too often we are wonderful to families until the funeral is over and then we drop them. Very few churches have an aftercare program.

The funeral experience is more than the service. It is entwined in a grieving process that lasts for many months. People judge the funeral by the whole experience. If we fail the family after the funeral, the memory of the event is marred.

If the clergy could attend a few of the conferences that I attend and hear the hurt and anger I hear, there would be a renewed interest in the funeral and in helping families face their grief.

CHAPTER 11

The Challenge of Changing Religious Patterns

America has long been described as a "Christian" nation. We earned that title by census figures rather than by our behavior, but it has always been understood that roughly half of our population are affiliated to some degree with a religious faith. The "Christian" is a misnomer. Fifty percent of our people are connected with a faith of their choice. All faiths must be included to attain that percentage. I do not know whether the next census will sustain that, nor do I know how many of that majority are affiliated in name only. Many have not actually attended the church of their choice since childhood.

On the surface it would appear that there is a great resurgence of religious interest going on in our country. Mega-churches that attract people by the thousands are springing up in most cities. We see their television broadcasts and hear glowing reports of the vast crowds that flock to each service, and are convinced that the entire country is in the middle of a great revival.

I am not sure the presence of these large church bodies indicates a growth in the percentage of our people who are active in a faith. It probably represents the fact that we, like Wal-Mart, are consolidating the church into larger and larger groups at the expense of the smaller ones. Someone has said that instead of being "fishers of men," we are keepers of the aquarium and we spend most of our time swapping fish.

Even if the next census allows us to keep our status as a nation of faith, it will only mean that at least fifty percent of our people are involved in a church. That means there is another fifty percent who are not so involved. That means that half of the people served by any funeral home will not have any affiliation with a religious body. Many of those included in the religious majority will be members by birth or name only. Many others will have an affiliation but have long ago become disillusioned and have dropped out completely. Right now, even though we are considered a religious nation, the majority of the people we serve do not have a church, synagogue, or mosque they can call home.

If the majority of the families served by a funeral home are Catholic, the funeral home takes the steps necessary to provide a Catholic service. If the majority of the families are Chinese or any other ethnic group, the funeral home learns how to provide funerals that fit the culture. This is just basic business sense.

Over half of our families are not religious, and we have nothing to offer them except a service that is religiously based. The family must select or find a clergy person whether they want one or not. Often they are ashamed about their lack of activity in a church. Often they find the ceremonies and messages strange instead of comforting. Too often funeral homes are designed as smaller versions of the church. The decorations, the music, the atmosphere is aimed at the faithful. Those with no religious affiliation are left without a funeral that fits and memorializes their life.

The pattern is that people leave the church but they return for funerals and weddings. Gradually they stop returning for funerals and weddings. Then they stop having these ceremonies at all.

Right now the highest rate of cremation and immediate dispositions is in the part of the U.S. and Canada with the lowest percentage of people who attend church. The Northwest part of both the United States and Canada have both the lowest percentage of church attendance and the highest rate of immediate dispositions. People who are not connected to a faith are by far the most likely candidates for little or no funeral.

We are beginning to feel the impact of this in every area of the continent. We are not experiencing the full impact as yet and will not for several more years. Right now we are burying the parents of the Baby Boomers and those who happen to die young. The Baby Boomers have enough of a connection with their faith to return for weddings and funerals. They went to church when they were young, and although most have stopped attending, they still count themselves as members. The next generation is called Generation X. These are the children of the Baby Boomers. At a recent church conference it was stated by good authority that 80% of Generation X have never been inside of a church. When it is their turn, we will be in the middle of the natural pattern of not having funerals and weddings.

Even though the full impact of this pattern is a generation away, we cannot wait until it is here to prepare for the challenge. Facing this challenge will require such a radical change in our thinking and funeral practice that it will take a generation to become ingrained as the norm. If we continue to lead the Baby Boomers to immediate disposition that will become the natural choice for all generations to come.

The question then becomes, what can be done to meet the needs of the people with no church? If there is action to be taken, who will begin the process?

SECTION III
MEETING THE
CHALLENGES

CHAPTER 12

Change Demands a Fresh Look at the Product

I am tired of suffering from the "paralysis of analysis." I am tired of making speeches and hearing speeches that are full of theories about what is wrong, but have no solutions to offer. It is way past time for us to concentrate on the practical steps we can take to meet the challenges facing funeral service. These steps will need to be deeper than some new marketing scheme or advertising program. These steps must encompass the whole of what we offer to families.

I would love to gather a group of the best thinkers in funeral service in a hotel room, lock the door for several days and brainstorm until we could list the challenges we face and the actions we need to take to face each challenge. I have begun planning a series of seminars that will be "thinks tanks" for this purpose. I am looking forward to the discoveries that will be unearthed in that environment. Until that day, all I can do is imagine the scene and share that vision.

We would dissect every facet of the funeral experience. We would study the history of how we started the traditions of the funeral. We would examine the attacks with open minds hoping to find reasons for the negative opinion of the press. By the end of discussion, there would be nothing left to examine, and we would be exhausted. I can envision someone standing in the middle of the room and saying, "Okay, What can we do? What will it take? What steps are going to be necessary to meet these challenges?"

I certainly don't have all of the answers. All I can report on is what I would say if asked that question. The first statement I would begin with is:

We Must Improve the Product
Build It and They Will Come

When we make the funeral into a meaningful experience, people will want to have funerals. All is not lost. We are not going out of business. We are not without hope. We can turn the tide back to families wanting all we have to offer instead of as little as they have to buy.

I have seen this work in my own ministry. I started studying the funeral in the late seventies. From that time on I have worked at making every funeral a personalized memorial to a life. The moment I began doing so, I became the person of choice for every city I served. Families who never attended any church would almost automatically ask for me to conduct the funeral for their loved one. I don't say that to brag, I say it as proof that people will have funerals if they are meaningful to their lives.

I have had the privilege of touring Australia and New Zealand. The trip to New Zealand entailed traveling around the entire country so I had the chance to study funeral service there in great detail. I learned that funeral service there faced some of the same problems we face. Although it was from a different cause, they were faced with the loss of business just as we are.

Their problems came from a strange source. The cemeteries in New Zealand belong to what we would call the county or the parish. The cemeteries also had the only licensed crematoriums. These crematoriums featured large chapels where a majority of the funerals were held. The funeral directors realized that all the crematoriums needed to take over funeral service completely was a preparation room. They needed something to make their work necessary and appreciated.

I could spend a great deal of time talking about all of the things they did to meet their challenge. I will not do so, but there are a few of them that are so germane to our situation that they must be noticed.

They Bound Themselves Together

They are competitive of course, but they saw this as a problem they all must work together to solve. Groups of them traveled to other countries to explore funeral service possibilities. They worked to find solutions. They developed a very strong educational program on a national scale.

They Developed Meaningful Ceremonies

New Zealand has an 80% cremation rate. They have a 100% funeral rate, and have never heard of immediate disposition. As the committal service died out, they devised beautiful closing ceremonies for cremation funerals. They made what could have been an awkward ending into a meaningful experience.

They Began Offering Receptions

There is now a reception following almost every funeral. The funeral homes have a reception hall or, in some cases, they use a nearby church. When the funeral is over, the family moves to the reception hall for a time of light refreshment and fellowship with their friends. The reception halls are so popular that several funeral directors have said that families often book the reception before they do the funeral.

They Personalized Their Service

I came away with the sense that these folks understood the most important thing they had to sell was the personal touch of the funeral director who served them. They offer service and folks respond.

I am not saying we must do what they do in New Zealand. I tell their story to make the point that trends can be turned around by making the product into something someone wants. We must discover innovations that fit our clients.

We need to:

Develop New Ceremonies

We need to be on the lookout for ways to create new ceremonies. An example of this need would be a ceremony of closure for cremation funerals. The first time I conducted a cremation funeral I sat in the parking lot for twenty minutes after the service was over. There was not a procession to the cemetery, and no committal service. It didn't end, we just quit. I understood why we did not do those things, but I needed something to take their place.

The experience left me cold and with a void inside.

Why not build a ceremony out of the current trend toward placing personal items in the casket? More and more families want to do this, but they think they must slip the items in at the funeral home before the service or when no one is looking before the casket is closed. If this practice has meaning for the family, it will have much more meaning if we make it into a ceremony. Funeral homes should have some practical items that could be used for this purpose on hand at the funeral home.

A friend confessed to me that he had left a bottle of Jack Daniels in the casket of his friend. He said they had shared many good times and told many lies with a bottle like that. I recognize that he would not do that in public, but he could have done so in a ceremony with the friends and family.

The possibilities for ceremony are endless. Finding ways to work them into the funeral is the next step. At the end of this chapter I want to outline a funeral that includes these experiences.

Discover the Value of Music

Music has the possibilities of transforming the funeral. If people are looking for an experience, the best way to provide that experience is through the intelligent use of music. It is an untapped resource we can no longer afford to miss.

We can no longer afford to be without the necessary equipment to produce a great musical presentation. I dream of the time when we will be able to present a medley of the person's favorite songs as part of the service. This can be done in addition to the church soprano singing with the Hammond organ. With modern equipment a medley can be put together in minutes and played as part of the service presented by the funeral home itself.

The major criticism this idea receives is, "Won't that make them cry?" My answer is "I certainly hope so." They came there to cry. Crying is part of the healing. It is time folks were crying because the music moved them, rather than because it hurt their ears.

We need music at the cemetery. Is it any wonder people are choosing cremation? Maybe they have had it with the cemetery experience. We stand out in the heat or the cold for a committal service we cannot hear. There are now wireless systems that can be mounted in the hearse.

All that is needed is to place the speakers and turn on the wireless mike. The speaking can be heard, and the system has the ability to play CDs or tapes. We need to either make the service meaningful or stop having it.

Discover Ways to Involve the Funeral Director in the Service

We have stood in the back of the room far too long. It is time for the funeral director to become a vital part of the service itself. We complain about how the clergy perform, and yet we dump the whole thing into their laps and add very little. I think the funeral director should be the master of ceremonies at the funeral. He or she could welcome the friends and express the appreciation of the family for their presence and care. The master of ceremony could introduce the musicians. Far too often they are hidden and the audience spends most of the service wondering who is singing. The minister or speaker could be introduced as well. Those in the audience who are from out of town will not know who is speaking. Often the speaker is from out of town and not well known. When I mention this idea I am usually asked what the clergy will think of the idea. I cannot imagine a clergy person or anyone else objecting to being introduced before they speak. It is a great help to any speaker.

A MODEL

With just these ideas in mind maybe we should build a model of what a funeral could look like. This is a very simple model. One that does not require any massive changes. Sometimes I think we present the need for change in such dramatic terms that we are left thinking we must change everything at once. What I am advocating is addition, not subtraction. I want to keep the traditional funeral intact. Families are comfortable and comforted by these traditions. All we need to do is add some meaningful moments to the funeral as we know it.

The model I am presenting here is very simple. It is the traditional funeral with some music and a ceremony added. We need to start simple and move slowly. We need to be careful not to scare or upset our families. This model will do neither.

This is only one model. We should be collecting ideas for other models from every person possible.

Master of Ceremonies. This person should be the funeral director who is serving the family. I recognize that not everyone is comfortable in front of people. If this funeral director is not, then some other staff person can fill the role. I think it is imperative that this person be a representative of the funeral home.

Introduction to the Service and Family Appreciation
Master of Ceremonies

Presentation of the Musical Tribute
The master of ceremonies would say something like: *"The music we love tells a great deal about a person. It is the meaning of the music and not the style that speaks. The lyrics, the words, and most important of all, the experiences the music is tied to. It may be a song played at a wedding. It may be a hymn learned long ago and loved for a lifetime. It may be a sad song heard playing at a low time. The music of a life shares meaningful memories. Listen for a few moments to the selections the family shared with us. This is the music of the life of _____.*

A ten minute medley plays.
There is a computer program called Power Point. Pictures can be scanned into this program and choreographed to the music to be shown as the music plays. There are also companies that will blend music and pictures on video to be shown during this part of the service.

The Obituary *(If one is to be used)*
Clergy /Speaker/Celebrant

Song
This is where the normal music of the service is used.

Scripture, Prayers or Comments
Clergy/Speaker/Celebrant

Words from Family or Friends
This is a growing practice and one that should be encouraged.
The master of ceremonies or the clergy can direct.

Another Song *(if needed)*

Eulogy Message
Clergy/Speaker/Celebrant

Closing Ceremony
Since I have only mentioned the need for such a ceremony, I need to interject some words of explanation here.

Logistics: We think this service is more effective if it is set apart from the rest of the funeral and participated in by only the family.

If used as the closing ceremony for a cremation funeral it might be more meaningful if the family rose and stood at the front of the room around a table with a picture of the loved one or the casket if the body is present.
An alternative would be for the family to stand at their seats.

In this sample we are including some religious statements. There will be that rare family that will not want any reference made to belief or God. In those cases these areas should be deleted. I have italicized those areas.

This should be printed and handed to the family with brief instructions about when they are to respond. When the speaker has concluded the message the master of ceremonies would move the family to the front. This is an ideal time to offer the family a chance to speak if they wish. It is also a great chance for a public ceremony of placing items in the casket if one is present, or on a table by the urn.

The Master of Ceremonies would say. *From as far back as time is recorded it has been the custom of many people to leave personal items with the loved one. Often this has been done out of superstition and fear. Often out of profound faith in the future. We are seeing both a revival and a change in this practice among people today. We now seem to feel the need to place some memento with the loved one, but we do so as a memorial to their lives and not as some superstitious act. The family may now present those mementoes if they wish.*

Then the master of ceremonies will lead the family in a responsive reading similar to this.

Leader: We live on in two ways. We live on in life beyond life. *We live on in eternal life with our God.* And we live on in the lives and memories of those we have loved. No one is dead until they are forgotten. How will we ever forget the impact and love of this life lived among us?

Family: We will remember

Leader: As each season changes from the chill
of winter to the warmth of spring. And
from the blue skies of summer to the
exploding colors of fall. In all
seasons…

Family: We will remember

Leader: It may be a dawn when the day is
awakening
Or during a quiet lull at the middle of
the day
Or at some unexpected moment when
your memory comes crashing into my
consciousness
And always during the lonely nights.
During every day…

Family: We will remember

Leader: For the examples lived among us
For the lessons taught and learned
For the concern felt about us
For the love shared with us
For each touch of your hand
For each smile you sent our way
For every word of encouragement that
lifted our spirits
For all that you were to us…

Family: We will remember

Leader: We will remember the times of joy
We will remember the times of pain
We will remember those quiet times of peace
And we will remember the grief of parting
In all our emotions...

Family: We will remember

Leader: Because we will remember, we do not say good-bye. We trust our loved one into the hands of our maker knowing that death is but passage into life beyond life. We do so knowing we will sorrow because they are gone, but we will rejoice forever because they lived.

If the funeral is led by a clergy person or a celebrant the leader could then call on this person to present their normal closing remarks to close the service. If no clergy is present, the leader could lead in prayer if that is appropriate or simply say, "Amen," "Shalom," or whatever statement seems needed to signify the end. A simple statement of, "And thus do we honor the memory of _____." will suffice.

If this ceremony takes place at the grave site then the normal service of committal would be appropriate.

That is a very simple model. It is a start. As we grow and develop, other ideas will be added. All we are trying to accomplish is a more personalized experience for the family. A personalized funeral does not have to be a dramatic departure. Little things can make a profound difference. My hope is that everyone who reads this will think of a better model. If we do so, we will be giving the funeral the thought it is going to need to survive.

CHAPTER 13

Change Will Demand
a New Role

It is apparent that this kind of model will demand a new role for the funeral director. Funeral directors are not accustomed to being up front and active in the funeral. They are the most comfortable standing unseen in the back of the room. I think some of the criticism about cost comes from the fact that nothing the funeral director does is seen by the family. All they see is a nice building and some very nice transportation. Neither of these are noticed very much while the funeral process is happening.

I hope to start a new profession within funeral service. I want to train some people in each funeral home as Bereavement Consultants. This does not mean additional personnel, anyone within the funeral home could take the training. These people would not necessarily become grief counselors, though some would also do the follow-up programs of the funeral home. The pre-need counselors might also be some of the best people to train as Bereavement Consultants. Any employee who does not mind speaking in public can be trained as a Bereavement Consultant.

The Bereavement Consultants would represent the funeral home by leading conferences and making speeches about grief in the community. They would become involved in hospice. They would present programs for Compassionate Friends and church groups. There is an ever growing interest in this subject and we need people in the communities who can meet the interest. It is not enough nor is it effective to bring in some outside speaker once every year or so to speak to some large gathering. This education process needs to be ongoing and it needs to be local.

If I were the owner of a funeral home, I would use the Bereavement Consultant as an initial contact with families. During first call, or when a call came in, I would say, "Our home offers the services of a Bereavement Consultant free of charge to every family we serve. This person does not arrange the funeral nor do they sell anything at all. They simply visit with your family about the grieving process and offer some wonderful help to your family as you face this loss. May I send this person by your home this afternoon for a short visit?" This allows some very helpful education to happen before the family comes to the funeral home for the arrangement conference. A contact with the family by a warm person trying to help them understand the grieving process can break down barriers, and begin the process of establishing the significance of a loved one.

I think the funeral director must become more of a consultant without taking over from the family. That may be a fine line, but it can be learned and walked quite easily.

Personal involvement is one of the great gifts the funeral has to offer to a family. If we do not show them how or lead them into the process, the family will never experience this gift. They have no idea what possibilities are available nor how to even begin to organize the funeral. Since the normal stance of the funeral director now is, "hands off and give the family anything they ask for," not much is asked for.

Sometimes the family will know the songs they want, but most have no idea what other personalization ideas are available to them. The funeral director needs to move into this vacuum.

This will be quite similar to the role I have played in wedding planning. In these cases the bride knows what she wants, and if she doesn't, her mother certainly does. Far too often the bride and her mother are at loggerheads over the plans. Some of the plans they come up with sound good but, from experience, I know they don't translate into real life very well at all. In weddings the thing to avoid are those awkward moments when no one knows what to do. Such moments happen when the couple want a song sung during some ceremony, such as lighting a candle, and the song lasts far longer than the ceremony. The couple stand there in panic wondering what to do next. It feels more awkward than it is, but these are the things a consultant tries to avoid.

I never asked for the job of wedding consultant. It was dumped on ministers when florists got smart and stopped doing this work for free. The clergy are still free, so we get to spend far too much time trying to get it just right. The positive thing that came out of my years of performing this thankless task is that I know how to consult without taking over.

I begin by letting the couple talk through their plans. I listen very carefully to the entire story. If I listen and don't interrupt, this does not take long. If I interrupt, the conversation gets off track and it takes about twice as long. After I have heard them out I simply say, "Since I have done a lot of weddings, maybe it would help if I told you some things others have tried that seemed to be meaningful to them. Understand that I have no preference for any of these ideas. All I want is your wedding to be exactly what you want." Then I list some creative ideas that folks have come up with that personalized their weddings.

I then tell them the things that tend to complicate a wedding. I tell them how to work through the awkward moments, and when the natural breaks are for injecting a song, etc.

The strange thing is, this sets them free. The more they talk, the more excited they get and the more ideas they discover. It becomes a time of creativity. I have helped that to happen and have not taken over in any way.

This same procedure will work with families in grief. First, we need to let them talk. Let them tell their story. Remember a safe place is also one of the other great gifts we give. They will usually tell how the person died, how they felt, and begin to tell who the person was and how much they are going to be missed.

The funeral director then, and only then, begins to say. "Our purpose is to plan just the right service you want as a gift to your loved one. I am not here to sell you anything nor pressure you in any manner. My job is to show you some of the things I have seen others do just to let you know what kinds of things can be done. These are things the family does. They are not things that I sell to you nor do they cost you anything. The best memorials are the ones that come from the creativity and love of the family."

Some examples that might be shared are the use of picture boards, the use of unusual but meaningful songs, displaying items that had great meaning for the person, placing items into the casket, and the possibility of some members of the family speaking a short word.

I do this with families, and have done so for years. I have never had a family think I was being pushy. As a matter of fact, most of the time it turns the family loose and quite often they really get into the process. This produces some unusual funerals, but it also produces funerals that have meaning and are remembered.

I remember one family where the grandchildren had been especially close to the grandfather. He was a painter and most of them had worked with him at one time or another. When we got together for the story telling time I always do with families before the funeral, they began to tell some of the funniest stories I have ever heard. When I asked them how they wanted to memorialize their grandfather, they took off. At the funeral they all gathered around the piano and sang many old songs. This is one of the things they always did at his house. They ended up with the loudest version of *I'll Fly Away* I think I have ever heard.

That funeral happened more than eight years ago. Anytime I meet a member of that family, they tell me again how much it meant and how they all still talk about Grandpa's funeral. Funerals like that do not just happen. Someone must be the consultant that guides families into a meaningful experience.

The model also calls for the funeral director to be more proactive in the actual funeral service. This is a departure from the norm, and many funeral directors will not be comfortable with having to be in front of people. Almost every funeral home will have at least one person who is very comfortable speaking before a group. This person could be utilized in a large number of the funerals directed by other staff members. There are ways to work this out if the idea becomes viable and desirable to a funeral home.

There will also need to be a new type of cooperation between the funeral director and the clergy. The clergy should not be sold short in this area. The majority of the clergy want to help people and will do so if we are given the proper instructions and chance. Almost every funeral director has one curmudgeon clergy person to deal with.

This person is usually very demanding and hard to please, but the rest of the clergy should not be painted with the same brush. If we change funeral service it will mean the funeral directors will need to get over their fear of the clergy and start communicating with them. A personal visit to discuss the defining of roles would do wonders. Some clergy will want to be in control of the entire service if it is held in their church, but some would welcome a master of ceremony and closing ceremony led by the funeral director. This would be especially true if they understood the materials in this book. This book was written in the hope that both groups would read and discuss it fully. Families are at stake, of course, but the ministry and service of both the clergy and the funeral director is also at stake.

Chapter 14

Change will Demand New Services

Many funeral directors have never had to plan and attend a funeral from a distance, and have very little knowledge of what kind of experience the family must face. Experienced or not, it is not impossible for someone to simply sit down and walk in the shoes of the families in their minds. That may be the best way to start facing this challenge. We need to have some grasp of what the family is facing before we can respond with very much interest or zeal.

Imagine what it must be like to go back to a home town you left forty-five years ago to plan a funeral for your parent. The parent has been in a nursing home for the last two years and the home has been sold. Your visits home have been consumed with giving care to the parents, so you have maintained very little contact with any friends in the town. You have no idea what is proper in a funeral. You have planned one for the other parent, and have attended a few, but there is no understanding of what can or should happen in a funeral. You have even less of a clue about what kind of funerals are proper in your home town. You left years ago and when you lived here you did not attend very many funerals.

Your parent has a pre-need program at the local funeral home, but you have no idea what that involves nor how it works. Does that mean you must use that particular home? Does that mean you have no choices about what happens in the service? You are the one in charge and you now know what is meant by the blind leading the blind.

To make matters worse, the rest of the family will not arrive in time to help with the plans, but you have one sister that will not like whatever plans you make and will make a scene when she finally arrives. You do not know your family as well as you would like. Since they all have scattered across the world, your contacts with them have been brief and seldom. Now you must make plans with and for family members you barely know. There is no place to visit in private with the family members who have arrived. What do they want done? How do they feel about things? What do they want to spend?

It is ten o'clock and time to go to the funeral home to make the arrangements.

Now, while you are imagining, think of ways to make this experience easier and more meaningful. That is where we must start. We must learn to be sensitive to the special needs of those who come to us from afar.

Remember the Little Things

A business owner passed out buttons at a conference where I was speaking. The buttons said, "I Make Sure." In his speech to the employees he said, "Quality is making sure. It is taking care of the small details." I like that idea. If we notice small needs and meet them, we produce quality care.

Small needs could include such things as a list of motels, florist, restaurants, cleaners, drug stores, baby sitting services, and any other service idea you can come up with. This list should be made available to the primary family member who will be called by the other family members. It should be printed so it can be faxed, emailed, or simply read over the phone to the family members who call.

I know one funeral director whose firm is in a small town with no motels. He bought a garage to use in his business and refurbished the apartment that was part of the garage. He makes the apartment available to families who are coming in for funerals. He reports glowingly of the responses he receives for his service.

Perhaps a Time to Think

It may be that the first thing we need to offer such families is a time and place to think. We might say, "I recognize that most of the family has just arrived and you probably have not had much time to talk among yourselves about what you wish to do in the funeral. There are so many interruptions at a time like this and it is hard to find a quiet place and time to talk together. May I suggest that you take a few moments now before we start making any plans. You can talk and think together about how you wish to memorialize the life of your loved one. I will be right outside the door if you have any questions that I can answer." Then leave them alone for a time.

Just the fact that you recognized the need will have meaning to the family. The quiet place of privacy will be most welcome.

These are just a few of the ideas we could come up with to try to make the experience less of a hassle and more of a time of memorialization.

Don't Let Them Slip Through Your Fingers

Families need a reason to return for funerals. They need a reason to use your home when they do return. Any contact you can maintain should be looked upon as something you must do. Keep a mailing list of these families and send them your calendar each year.

Since I produce the aftercare program for The Dodge Company, I am prejudiced, but I think the scattering of society makes an aftercare program an absolute necessity. The positive reviews of these programs show the help they give to families and the appreciation the families feel. We get calls almost daily from families who have received the books and want to order additional copies for other family members. The things they say about the funeral home that sent the books to them prove my point beyond any doubt. These people will remember the funeral home that helped them.

The Role of the Clergy

The clergy can provide a wonderfully healing service to these scattered families. Usually they do not know the clergy person who is going to do the service. They hardly know each other and find it hard to communicate across long forgotten lines of relationships. For years I have gotten the family together for a time of story telling. I talk about this in more detail later, but this is even more needed and appreciated when the family is gathering from afar. An hour of sharing stories can be the best work a minister does. It breaks down the barriers and begins the process of grieving together for the family. It also makes the funeral itself much easier and more personal.

A New Idea of Service

The books I have written on grief are designed as gift books. People buy them to give to friends and loved ones when a death occurs. We have regular customers who purchase these books a dozen at a time and give them every time a death happens. I have observed this for years and wondered how to make it easier for people to get access to these and other products that will help a friend face their grief. There is now a new idea in funeral service that will make that possible. Many funeral homes are beginning to feature a small and very tasteful gift area. These areas feature books, cards, and memorializing gifts. The idea is shocking at first, but then you realize that hospitals have had gift shops for years and no one is offended by their presence. As a matter of fact they find these to be a great convenience.

My company, In-Sight Books, and other companies such as York Casket started promoting the idea. It has taken a little bit of adjustment but it has become evident this is an idea whose time will come. Even though I was involved in starting the idea, I had no idea how helpful these centers could be until I attended the funeral for my wife's uncle in Arizona. As I related earlier, we arrived late afternoon the day before the funeral the next morning. We had not purchased any flowers, cards, nor any memorializing gift. I prefer to give books, but there was no place to find the books I needed. I spent the next morning in a mad dash trying to find a florist that would deliver a spray in time for the funeral. Our scattered society has opened up a service we can fill. We can offer these families the convenience of a gift center and helpful products to walk with them through their grief or to memorialize a life. One of the highest priority needs is to establish the significance of the person. A gift that can help that is welcomed and healing.

CHAPTER 15

Change will Demand a New Level of Comfort

The greatest need by far in both funeral service and among the clergy is to expand our comfort zones. Most of the problems we have in giving care to people comes from our own fears in dealing with people in pain. One of the great surprises of my life was finding out how deep this fear is.

A minister approached me at a conference recently and said, "I have been assigned the task of grief follow-up in our church. Can you tell me what I can do to help these people?" It became evident that he was not going to be comfortable with leading any kind of grief group, so I told him about a follow-up program we have for churches and hospices to use. It is very similar to the one we produce for funeral homes and consists of four books that are mailed throughout the first year. He was interested until I suggested that he should write a brief note to include with each book. He almost grabbed me by the lapel and with a shaky voice said, "Will you write those notes for me?" He had been a pastor for many years and yet the idea of writing a note to the bereaved scared him until he was shaking.

I am sure that pastor is not unique. No one prepares us for this work. None of our training tells us how to talk to people in pain. The funeral directors are also untrained in this area and are also frightened at the prospect. That sounds strange since most of them deal with people in grief all day every day. But the fear is there none the less. It may be well hidden, but it is there.

This fear causes pastors to not follow up with families after the funeral. They don't know what to say so they delay going, the delay stretches out until it is too late to go, and the family feels the pastor does not care. This same fear has gradually diminished the personal touch of the funeral director down to simply walking the family through the filling out of a form. We make it all set and simple so we won't have to deal with the things we are not comfortable being around.

If I had a "funeral school" the first class would be on listening to people in pain. The class would not just deal with the mechanics of listening nor the study of body language. The class would try to show what happens to a person when they are heard. The insights that come as someone listens to us. The learning that happens as we talk. The healing found in having someone who is trying to simply understand us. How great it feels to have our thoughts legitimized and our feelings given credence. It is amazing what happens to a person when they are heard. If we could understand that we would be well on our way to comfort.

It is hard getting comfortable just listening. We think we have not done anything until we have said something. We think the person we are talking with will think we are stupid or have no answers. Just the opposite is true. I cannot relate how many times a person in counseling has told me how much help they have received from some session where I wondered if I was wasting the person's time.

I always end up saying the same thing—people in grief need the three H's. They need us to *Hang Around, Hug Them, and Hush.* We need to learn how to trust presence, trust touch, and, most of all, trust silence. If we know that, we can serve without fear.

We also need to get comfortable with the effectiveness of what we offer to families. We need to form a course of study I would call the "Anatomy of a Funeral." This would entail taking each little part of what we do for families and having a dissecting session. We need to look at why we do what we do. Where did the practice originate? What purpose does it have now? From the first call to the aftercare program, we need to understand why we do each step and what that step is doing for families. These things are not just old habits we can't get rid of. They have an impact on the grieving process of a family and we need to know that impact.

The same is true of the clergy. We do funerals almost by rote with very little understanding of what each part can do to help. If we were asked a simple question like, "Is it good for a family to cry at a funeral or should we try to help them keep the tears under control?" Most of us would not know how to answer that question and would not know any source that could tell us the answer.

It is no wonder then that we spend our lives fighting off feelings of inadequacy and fear around folks in pain.

CHAPTER 16

Everyone Needs a Funeral

In November of 1999, my company produced our first training session for funeral Celebrants in Newton, Massachusetts. The second such training was held in Toronto and many more will follow. When people find out that a minister is trying to start a movement to provide secular funerals for people who have no religious connections, they think I have left both my faith and my senses. The answer is quite simple. I believe in the funeral. I think funerals should be available to every family. I also think the funeral should be personal to the person who has died. The most nonreligious person alive deserves and needs a funeral that eulogizes his or her life.

The funeral is not necessarily a religious service. It certainly can be very religious and should be so if the person was a follower of that religion. But a nonreligious person should not be forced to have a religious service just because that is all that is available to the family. It has become my belief that we must learn how to offer funerals that fit where people are. To do that, we must have Celebrants who will deliver secular funerals.

The Celebrants do not have to be nonreligious themselves. As a matter of fact, we have had many ministers and nuns go through the training already. When I learned that four nuns and an assistant to a priest had signed up for our first seminar, I almost panicked. I thought maybe they misunderstood what we were doing and would be greatly turned off by the experience. To my amazement they understood very well and saw this as a great opportunity of service and outreach. As they put it, if we minister to a family at a time like this we have served them as we are called to do. We also have a much better chance of reaching them in the future. Some of our most enthusiastic celebrants are nuns and ministers.

A Celebrant funeral is not an anti-God service. In New Zealand and Australia where the idea was born, the Celebrant asks the family what they want sung and read. In a large majority of cases they want *How Great Thou Art* sung and *Psalm 23* read. Most of these folks are not against God, they just haven't found a church where they fit.

A Celebrant is a person who seeks
to meet the needs of families during their
time of loss. They serve by providing
a funeral service that is personalized to reflect
the personality and life style
of the deceased.

The credo of the Celebrant must be that every person needs and deserves a funeral. Every life is worthy of being memorialized and that we best serve their families when we provide a fitting funeral ceremony.

A Celebrant is certified by taking training sessions that are accredited by a major university. The training consists of one weekend introductory course to be followed by more advanced training in the future.

When the courses start, the Celebrants usually express great doubt about their qualifications. I tell them that by the time the weekend is over they will have spent more time actually studying the funeral process than any minister they know and probably any funeral director they know.

We start on Friday night and close on Sunday morning. By Sunday morning the celebrants are delivering eulogies that anyone would be proud to have for a loved one. If every funeral was as well done as the ones these folks have produced, our problems would be over. People would want funerals.

The program should work by the trained Celebrant contacting several funeral homes and being available to conduct funerals for those families who have no clergy. When a family comes in, the funeral director makes the connection between the family and the Celebrant who seems to fit the family the best. Our hope for the future is that every funeral home will have the choice of several Celebrants.

The Celebrant goes to the home and directs the family in what I call the story time. After the story time, the funeral is quite easy. The Celebrant can incorporate into the service what the family expressed about the person by telling these stories. This produces a very personalized funeral that leaves the family feeling blessed indeed.

The Celebrant training has a strong emphasis on ethics and practices. We ask funeral directors to also take the training to be a part of the discussion of a code of ethics and practices. We also think the training will be beneficial to funeral directors themselves. We do not expect many to become Celebrants although in Australia and New Zealand many funeral directors choose to be the Celebrant for their firm. We think the funeral director will learn a great deal from the training and from communicating with the Celebrants in training. Some funeral homes have paid the registration fees for members of their staff to attend so they would have a Celebrant always available.

The Celebrant idea could have a major impact on the future of funeral service in several ways. It has the potential of helping stem the tide of immediate dispositions. It is very easy to establish the fact that most of these come from families who have no church or clergy. As the Celebrant idea spreads and becomes more and more a normal alternative, I predict there will be many families who will decide to have a funeral.

Celebrants will have an impact by modeling well-done, personalized funeral services. As more and more people attend these services, the word will spread. The only way to affect change is to model the new idea. In New Zealand the church and the clergy were very set in the traditional Church Of England funeral. As the church membership and activity dropped, more and more families began to complain about the lack of an alternative to meet their needs. Finally a rabble rousing woman took on the issue. She began to write articles, appear in the media, and finally wrote a book demanding that the unchurched people be served. That led to the Celebrant movement in that country. The major impact has not only been that families have been served; the major impact has been on the clergy. As more and more people chose Celebrants, the clergy began to ask why. The answer was simple and the results were predictable. They had to start doing much better and more personalized funerals. Our hope is that this movement will have that same impact in the United States and Canada.

CHAPTER 17

Personalization is Not a Product

A funeral director in Oregon stopped me after a presentation and put his finger squarely on the problem we face. He said something like, "I know we must personalize the funeral and I really try, but after I have gotten the family to use a picture board what else is there for me to do?"

It is very evident that we must personalize the funeral. The options are personalize or trivialize. For when a funeral does not relate to the person who has died and does not reflect on that life, the family feels as if no one thinks the person mattered nor does the death matter. The person becomes one more funeral for all of us to go through and act like we care. This entire book has been aimed at the need to personalize the funeral. But...

...Personalization is an attitude, not a product

We cannot produce a personalized funeral by some group of activities or products we provide. There is a danger that we will try to do just that. I have heard personalization presented as a set number of steps for us to do and, bingo, we did it! Personalization begins in the attitude shown by the funeral directors and the person conducting the funeral. If we come across as tired and bored it will not matter whether there is a picture board or not. A few products cannot cover our disinterest in the person or the family.

...Personalization is the entire experience

That is a summation of all this book has to say. Every thing we do for a family as a funeral director or as a clergy person must convey a sense of empathy and care. From the first contact through the entire funeral and the aftercare we need to be in the business of helping the family establish the significance of the person and the loss.

It all begins at first call—There is no time more important than this and no time that has as much possibility of giving help to the family. I am sorry to report that more and more funeral homes have stopped even making this important contact with the family. Far too often when the call comes the funeral director tells the family they will pick the body up at a later time and makes an appointment for the next day. Too often clergy do the same thing and families are left untouched.

I know a funeral home that has been in business less than four years and has already had over 400 funerals. I asked the owner what was her secret and she began to tell me a wonderful story of personal touch service. **When a call comes in–they go**. They may not be able to pick up the body at that time but they are there. If the removal is from a home she folds the bed covers and places them on the foot of the bed. Then she places a satin rose on the covers. Those roses cost her about 40 cents at a hobby shop. There is no way to estimate how many funerals they have brought to her door.

She makes it a point to ensure that whoever makes the removal is present the next day to personally welcome the family and introduce them to the funeral director who will be in charge of the service. Little stuff means a lot.

It continues through the arrangement conference—When I hear such things as a funeral director bragging that he could do an arrangement in twenty minutes I just cringe. That means the family had no time to tell their story and the funeral director joined the long line of folks who are trivializing the experience for the family. They need to talk. They need to cry. They need to know it is all right to do so in front of the funeral director. It takes a little longer to do it right. Giving a little time is another of those little things that mean a lot.

Participation takes time—The family comes to us as rank amateurs. They don't know how to do funerals. Some won't even know what a funeral is. Most will have no idea what they can do to personalize the event. The funeral director serving as a consultant and simply listing possible ideas comes across to a family that someone really wants to present a fitting and meaningful memorial.

Little things at the service—A friend of mine loved old cars and old tractors. He had one of each that had been perfectly restored to their original form. The funeral director suggested to the family that these be parked outside the church for the funeral. When the family saw the car and tractor sitting there they were deeply moved. Even though they knew they were going to be there, they had no idea they would mean so much. They are still thanking that funeral director. It is not a big deal to get a tractor and a car driven to a church. It is big when the family sees them there.

A Worthy Production—It really doesn't take much work or much time to produce great music. The tools are readily available for almost limitless possibilities. It does take some time to prepare a personalized message, but it is not hard. A private time with the family where stories are told makes the presentation the next day almost automatic. Every personal story is worth a thousand other words to the family.

The committal—The graveside committal is one of my very pet soap boxes. These services just must be improved. It would be very easy and relatively inexpensive to have a speaker system available. A little thing everyone present will notice and talk about. The friend I wrote about in this chapter has revived the old lap robes that once were prevalent in funeral service. She reports that these are met with glowing reports.

She also found a man who raises homing pigeons. At the committal service after the minister has finished, she says a few words and, on cue, the pigeons are released. The cage is disguised so no one expects this event. The pigeons are home before the handler leaves the cemetery, but the family never quits talking about what those birds meant to them.

It does not end with the funeral—I almost quoted Yogi Bera and said "It ain't over until it's over." It is hard for me to imagine a funeral home with no aftercare program. The impact of these programs is so evident and the need so elementary I am embarrassed to have to mention the need. If a company can keep up with its customers, it is unthinkable that they would not do so. Especially if the company knew that the customer was going to need the services they sell on many other occasions.

Since this book will also be read by clergy persons, it gives me a chance to urge every church to follow up on the families in loss. The one complaint I hear over and over is that as soon as the funeral is over the church is through. No one says anymore about the loss. This just can't continue.

Lives are hurt by dynamic events that shatter the soul. They are healed by simple touches of small kindnesses.

CHAPTER 18

The Power of Presence

My first SIDS death call came when I was a very young minister. I had not only never heard of Sudden Infant Death Syndrome, I had never been called to help a family who had lost a child. A young mother had found her child dead in the crib. When I arrived her mother and other members of the family were there and I walked into chaos. The little boy was lying on the couch and the family members were physically restraining the mother to keep her from touching her baby. When I walked in they immediately said, "You must help us. She mustn't touch that baby. You must convince her to give him up." I had no idea whether she should touch the baby or not. I supposed they knew best and started toward the mother.

Just as I started walking someone said, "Mr. Lockstone is here." Mr. Lockstone was the funeral director in our town. A well-loved gentleman who had served the whole town for years. I wish I could recreate the feeling that swept that room. Suddenly everything was going to be all right. We were not alone. Someone was there who knew what to do. I cannot express the deep sense of relief I felt at that moment.